# BACKSTAGE PASS

## By Margaret Magnarelli

SCHOLASTIC INC.

Photo Credits:

Photographs copyright © 2014:

AP Images: Cover top left (Charles Sykes), 8 (Scott Kirkland/PictureGroup), 17 (Frank Micelotta),
19 (Jeff Daly/Invision), 20 (Matt Sayles), 25 (Leon/PictureGroup), 26 (Jordan Strauss),
27 (Dowling/PictureGroup), 33 (Andreas Branch/Patrick McMullan/Sipa USA),
34 bottom (Rex Features), 40 (Peter Kramer), 41 (Joel Ryan), 46 top, 46 center (Owen Sweeney),
46 bottom (Owen Sweeney/Invision), 48 (Jordan Strauss/Invision)

Corbis Images/Splash News: 43

Getty Images: Cover top right (Jason Kempin/WireImage), cover bottom (Toby Zerna/Newspix),
back cover center (Juan Naharro Gimenez), back cover left (Steve Granitz/WireImage),
1 (Kevin Mazur), 4 (Kevin Mazur/TCA 2011), 6 (Michael Buckner), 10 (George Pimentel/WireImage),
11 (Tommaso Boddi), 14 & 15 (Cindy Ord), 18 (Sonia Recchia/WireImage), 22 (Toby Canham),
23 (Jason LaVeris/FilmMagic), 28 (Peter Kramer/NBC/NBC NewsWire), 29 (Tyler Golden/NBC/NBCU
Photo Bank), 38 (James Lemke Jr),42 (Frazer Harrison), 44 (James Devaney/WireImage),
45 (Kevin Winter/DCNYRE2013), 47 (Steve Granitz/WireImage)

Newscom: 9 (PacificCoastNews), 31 (KH1 WENN Photos), 32 (INB WENN Photos),
35 top (KB4 WENN Photos), 35 center (JGM, PacificCoastNews),
35 bottom (Pete Mariner/Retna/Photoshot), 36 (Jen Lowery/Splash News),
37 (Scope/MCT), 39 (Peter West/ACE Pictures/ACE Pictures),

Retna Ltd./Rob Grabowski: 13

REX USA: 5 (Matt Baron/BEImages), 7 (Snap Stills), 12 (Jim Smeal/BEImages),
16 (Newspix), back cover right (Peter Brooker), 21 (Stewart Cook), 34 top (Matt Baron/BEImages)

Zuma Press/Globe Photos: 24 (D. Long), 30 (TLeopold)

© 2013 by Scholastic

ISBN 978-0-545-59132-4

Published by Scholastic Inc.
SCHOLASTIC and associated logos are trademarks and/or registered trademarks of Scholastic Inc.

12 11 10 9 8 7 6 5 4 3 2 1                                            13 14 15 16 17 18/0
Printed in the U.S.A.                                                              40
First printing, September 2013

# Contents

# Introduction

**W**ant an all-access backstage pass into the lives of your favorite actors and musicians? You've got it! On the pages that follow, you'll get the lowdown on the biggest rising stars under the age of thirty. Find out everything from their favorite foods and activities to how they got their big breaks and what inspires them. Plus, you'll get the inside scoop on what they'll be doing next!

# Asa Butterfield

## ★ STAR STATS ★

**Name:** Asa Maxwell Butterfield
**Birthday:** April 1, 1997
**Hometown:** Islington, London, England
**Parents:** Jacqueline Farr and Sam
**Butterfield**
**Siblings:** older brother, Morgan;
younger sisters Loxie and Marlie
**Hobbies:** reading; playing soccer
and rugby; attending music festivals;
playing piano, guitar, and drums

**A**sa Butterfield's acting career began early: He was just seven years old when he joined an afterschool program at the Young Actors Theatre in the London borough of Islington. Discovered soon after by a talent agent, Asa landed a few roles on British TV before making his big-screen debut in the 2008 film *The Boy in the Striped Pajamas*. In the movie, set during World War II, Butterfield plays the son of a Nazi officer who befriends a Jewish child imprisoned in a concentration camp. A few years later, he appeared in *Nanny McPhee*

*Returns*. What really catapulted him into fame, however, was his leading role in the 2011 movie *Hugo*. Not only did that job win him praise from critics, it also fostered his friendship with costar Chloë Grace Moretz.

What's next for the sixteen-year-old with the piercing blue eyes? Watch for Asa in the much-anticipated sci-fi film *Ender's Game*, based on the novel of the same name, which is scheduled to come out in late 2013. He'll play Ender, a prodigious teen who is hoped to be the salvation for humanity in an intergalactic war. A fan of the book, Butterfield has described the role as "incredible."

# Ross Lynch

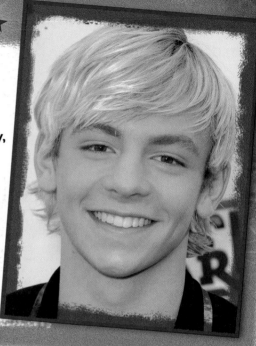

**Name:** Ross Shor Lynch
**Birthday:** December 29, 1995
**Hometown:** Littleton, Colorado
**Parents:** Mark and Stormie Lynch
**Siblings:** three brothers Riker, Rocky, and Ryland; one sister, Rydel
**Favorite Food:** Cadbury Crème Eggs
**Favorite Color:** yellow
**Favorite Movie:** *Romeo + Juliet*
**Hobbies:** playing music and ice hockey, flying model airplanes, drawing

**R**oss Lynch is a true triple threat: He's a musician, dancer, *and* an actor. Growing up in Colorado, Ross learned to sing and play music from his older siblings and by mimicking pop hits. Ross picked up the piano, drums, bass, and guitar this way. Back then, the Lynch kids would jam in their basement. When the family moved from Littleton to Los Angeles in 2007, the four eldest siblings — plus family friend Ellington Ratliff — got serious about music. They formed a

pop-rock act called R5, which signed with Hollywood Records in 2012. The group released an EP called *Loud* in early 2013.

Ross also has some sick dance moves. He's been dancing since he was five, and you may have seen him performing with The Rage Boyz Crew on *So You Think You Can Dance* in 2009. He's also the cousin of pro dancers Derek and Julianne Hough!

Somehow Ross also finds time to pursue acting. In 2011, he was cast as the title character Austin Moon in the Disney Channel series *Austin & Ally*. He plays a kid whose homemade music video makes him famous (um, Justin Bieber, anyone?). He's also appeared in *Teen Beach Musical*, a Disney Channel original movie.

# Bridgit Mendler

 **STAR STATS**

**Name:** Bridgit Claire Mendler
**Birthday:** December 18, 1992
**Hometowns:** Washington, DC, and San
Francisco, California
**Parents:** Harry and Leah Mendler
**Pets:** a dog named Missy
**Favorite Foods:** sushi, chocolate
**Favorite Musician:** Gavin DeGraw
**Favorite Book:** *Hamlet*

Talk about great beginnings: One of Bridgit Mendler's first major acting roles was as Nick Jonas's love interest on an episode of the Disney Channel show *Jonas*! That was in 2009, when she was sixteen. But Bridgit caught the acting bug several years earlier, after her family moved from Washington, DC, to the San Francisco area. She performed in a play, got hooked on acting, and eventually signed up with an agent.

Not long after appearing on *Jonas*, Bridgit scored a regular part on Disney's *Wizards of Waverly*

*Place.* Then, in 2010, she got her own show: *Good Luck Charlie.* (She also sang the theme song!) Other accomplishments include doing voiceovers for *The Secret World of Arrietty* and *Beverly Hills Chihuahua 2,* and starring in the TV movie *Lemonade Mouth.*

Haven't seen her on screen yet? Maybe you've heard her music. In 2012, she released an album, *Hello My Name Is...*; and her single "Ready or Not" made it onto the international top 40 charts. So far, 2013 has been an eventful year for Bridgit: Besides filming the fourth season of *Good Luck Charlie,* she began her freshman year at the University of Southern California and she's been touring for her album. Looks like this shining star is rising fast!

# Phillip Phillips

**Name:** Phillip LaDon Phillips, Jr.
**Birthday:** September 20, 1990
**Hometowns:** Albany, Georgia and Leesburg, Georgia
**Parents:** Sheryl and Phillip "Donnie" Phillips, Sr.
**Siblings:** two sisters
**Favorite Foods:** cube steak, fried chicken, meatloaf, mashed potatoes
**Favorite Musicians:** Jonny Lang, John Butler, Dave Matthews, Damien Rice, Mumford & Sons, Tool

*American Idol* winner Phillip Phillips has been playing guitar since he was fourteen, and credits his older sister's then-boyfriend Ben with teaching him his first chords. Years later, Phillip and Ben—who ended up marrying Phillip's sister—formed a band, which had some success booking local venues. Meanwhile, Phillip enrolled at Georgia's Albany Technical College to study industrial systems technology. After graduating, he went to work for his family's local business while continuing to make music on the side.

When he heard *American Idol* was hosting season 11 auditions in Savannah, Georgia in 2011, he decided to try out. Phillip wowed the judges with his initial songs and soon passed through to the semifinals.

While the show was filming, Phillip became severely ill due to kidney obstruction. In spite of this, he made it through the competition without ever being up for elimination. On May 23, 2012, he won against Jessica Sanchez in a record vote-casting. Phillip followed up his win with performances along the *American Idol* tour, and he began writing songs for his debut album. *The World from the Side of the Moon* dropped in November 2012. In 2013, he's toured both with Matchbox Twenty and on his own. Fans can't wait to hear more from this talented star!

# Debby Ryan

**Name:** Deborah Ann Ryan
**Birthday:** May 13, 1993
**Hometown:** Huntsville, Alabama
**Sibling:** older brother, Chase
**Pets:** a toy Poodle named Presley
**Favorite Foods:** tea, coffee, cottage cheese
**Favorite Movies:** *Talladega Nights*, the Indiana Jones series, the Star Wars series
**Hobbies:** reading, vintage shopping, writing a music blog, photography, and drawing

Debby Ryan got her first acting gig in Germany: Her dad, who's in the military, was stationed there, and the nine-year-old Debby had a part in a play on the base! By her early teens, her family had moved back to the States, and she started getting serious about the craft. Within a few years, her family relocated to Los Angeles for her career.

In 2008, Debby made her Disney Channel debut in *The Suite Life on Deck*, a spinoff of *The Suite*

*Life of Zack & Cody*. That show ran until 2011, when the network gave Debby her own show called *Jessie*, about a small-town girl who moves to New York City to become a nanny. Debby has also starred in several Disney Channel original movies, including *16 Wishes*, *The Suite Life Movie*, and *Radio Rebel*.

A self-described "nerd," Debby was a member of her high school's chess club and served as the school mascot! She's also an accomplished musician who sings, writes music, and plays guitar, piano, and keyboard. She's recorded songs for several of the Disney projects she's been involved in. Fashion is yet another passion: Not only does she have a YouTube series called *RyanStyle*, but she's also developing a clothing line!

# Taylor Swift

**Name:** Taylor Alison Swift
**Birthday:** December 13, 1989
**Hometowns:** Montgomery County, Pennsylvania, and Wyomissing, Pennsylvania
**Parents:** Andrea and Scott Kingsley Swift
**Sibling:** younger brother, Austin
**Pet:** a cat named Meredith
**Favorite Musicians:** Shania Twain, Faith Hill, the Dixie Chicks, Patsy Cline, Loretta Lynn, Tammy Wynette, Dolly Parton
**Hobbies:** songwriting, watching movies

Taylor Swift is a pop-country prodigy. She made her first studio album at just sixteen years of age. And last year, at just twenty-two, she released her fourth album, *Red*.

So far, she's won seven Grammys and six Country Music Association Awards, and she's taken home the Nashville Songwriters Association's Songwriter/Artist Award five times. She appeared in the 2010 movie *Valentine's Day* and voiced the role of Audrey in *The Lorax*, and she's written original music for a few films, too—including *The Hunger Games*. Not a bad resume for a twenty-three-year-old!

Taylor actually got her start in musical theatre while growing up in Pennsylvania. Over time, her interest shifted toward country music, and having dabbled in poetry, she also began working on songwriting. When she was fourteen, her family relocated to Nashville. Through a manager, she landed an artist development deal with RCA Records; then, at a talent showcase, she secured a contract with her current label, Big Machine Records.

She began touring for her new album *Red* in March, and she's also rumored to be working on a fifth album. Chances are her fans won't have to wait long to hear more from this spectacular songstress!

# Austin Mahone

**Name:** Austin Carter Mahone
**Birthday:** April 4, 1996
**Hometowns:** San Antonio, Seguin, and La Vernia, Texas
**Parent:** Michele Mahone
**Siblings:** none
**Pets:** two cats
**Favorite Foods:** pizza, lasagna, ziti, chicken alfredo, ice cream
**Favorite Color:** red
**Favorite Musicians:** Drake, Ne-Yo, Justin Bieber
**Hobbies:** playing and watching basketball, playing piano and drums, dancing

**W**hile attending high school in San Antonio, Texas, in 2010, Austin Mahone and his best friend, Alex, battled boredom by creating music videos. In the videos, the musical Mahone covers certain chart toppers, such as Justin Bieber's "Mistletoe" and Jason Mraz's "I'm Yours." The videos went viral, earning Austin a loyal following.

In late summer of 2012, Austin inked a deal to record an album. His first singles — "11:11,"

"Say Somethin," and "Say You're Just a Friend"—climbed the charts. And his June 2012 New York City concert sold out in less than an hour thanks to his dedicated fans, who call themselves "Mahomies."

The full album is due out in 2013, and Austin has been promoting it by touring with Taylor Swift, whom he first met a few years back in a café in Nashville. It's hard to believe that just three years ago Austin was a regular kid who played on his high school basketball and football teams. He says it's been a "huge journey" and that he can't believe how far he's come. His favorite quote seems to sum up his plans for the future: "Make the most of every opportunity because you only get one chance."

# Josh Hutcherson

## ★ STAR STATS ★

**Name:** Joshua Ryan Hutcherson
**Birthday:** October 12, 1992
**Hometown:** Union, Kentucky
**Parents:** Michelle and Chris Hutcherson
**Sibling:** younger brother, Connor
**Pets:** dogs Diesel, Nixon, and Driver; two cats
**Hobbies:** cooking; soccer; kickboxing; free-running; and following the Cincinnati Reds and Bengals, and the University of Kentucky Wildcats

Even before *The Hunger Games* came out in 2012, then-nineteen-year-old Josh Hutcherson had already made a name for himself in Hollywood. The Kentucky native had started acting at age nine, after a screen test he did convinced his parents to move to Los Angeles.

One of his first big roles was in the 2004 computer-animated film *The Polar Express*: He did voice and motion-capture acting for the lead character. He followed that up with a string of movies, and, of course, he plays Peeta Mellark in *The Hunger Games* and its 2013 sequel. And we'll definitely see more Peeta in the third and fourth installments of The Hunger Games movies as well!

# Jennifer Lawrence

Name: **Jennifer Shrader Lawrence**
Birthday: **August 15, 1990**
Hometown: **Louisville, Kentucky**
Parents: **Karen and Gary Lawrence**
Siblings: **older brothers Ben and Blaine**
Pets: **one dog, a Yorkie**
Hobbies: **painting, horseback riding, playing sports**

**B**ack in 2004, the girl who would one day become Katniss Everdeen was a cheerleader from Kentucky. Jennifer Lawrence's big break came while she was on spring break in New York with her family. Jen (as she's known to friends) was actually stopped on the street by a talent scout.

Jennifer has appeared in a number of indie films, and she won the Oscar for Best Actress in 2013. Playing Mystique in *X Men: First Class* and Katniss in *The Hunger Games* proved her a capable action heroine, too. In 2014, she'll appear in the sequel *X-Men: Days of Future Past*; and with *Mockingjay* being split into two parts, we'll be seeing a lot more of her as Katniss, too.

# Liam Hemsworth

★ STAR STATS ★

Name: **Liam Hemsworth**
Birthday: **January 13, 1990**
Hometown: **Melbourne, Victoria, Australia**
Parents: **Leonie and Craig Hemsworth**
Siblings: **older brothers Chris and Luke**
Pets: **five dogs**
Favorite Foods: **Krispy Kreme Doughnuts**
Favorite Movies: ***A Guide to Recognizing Your Saints**, **The Goonies**, **The Departed**, **Step Brothers**, **James Dean***

**L**iam's two older brothers are both actors, and he got an agent while in high school. He had parts in a few Australian TV shows before he shipped off to Hollywood in 2009. He came to the US to screen-test for the lead role in *Thor*, but he actually lost the part to his own brother Chris! (He says the competition between the siblings is friendly, though. Phew!)

Luckily for Liam, though, he soon landed the role of Gale Hawthorne in the first Hunger Games film. He's got several other projects coming out after *Catching Fire*, including playing Ali Baba in the 3D version of *Arabian Nights*, scheduled to come out in 2014.

# Sam Claflin

## ⋆ STAR STATS ⋆

**Name:** Samuel George Claflin
**Birthday:** June 27, 1986
**Hometown:** Ipswich, Suffolk, England
**Parents:** Mark and Sue Claflin
**Siblings:** older brothers Dan and Ben; younger brother, Joe
**Favorite Foods:** cheesy mashed potatoes, toad-in-the-hole with baked beans (a British specialty)
**Favorite Movie:** *The Goonies*

Sam makes his Hunger Games debut in *Catching Fire*. He plays Finnick Odair, a tribute who joins up with Katniss Everdeen and Peeta Mellark in the seventy-fifth Games. An avid soccer player, Sam had thought about pursuing pro "footie"—until he broke his ankle. A role in a school play gave him another aspiration, though, and he went on to complete coursework at The London Academy of Music and Dramatic Art.

After acting in a few British TV series and films, he got the role of Finnick. He says starring in *Catching Fire* has been a lot of pressure since fans of the series Tweet him to say he'd better not mess it up!

# Rachel Crow

**Name:** Rachel Kelly Crow
**Birthday:** January 23, 1998
**Hometown:** Mead, Colorado
**Parents:** Barbara and Kelly Crow
**Sibling:** younger sister, Hannah
**Pets:** a dog, Charlie
**Favorite Food:** chocolate
**Favorite Color:** light blue
**Favorite Books:** the Diary of a Wimpy Kid series, the Dork Diaries series
**Favorite Movie:** *Titanic*
**Hobbies:** swimming, karate, painting

Rachel Crow is off to a super career as a singer and actress. After her debut as a contestant on the American version of *The X Factor* in 2011, the year 2012 saw the release of her debut EP *Rachel Crow*. She also toured with Big Time Rush, sang the national anthem at the White House Easter Egg Roll, and guest-starred on Nickelodeon's *Fred: The Show*. She's also reportedly working on her own series for Nick.

This feisty five-foot phenom has come a long way, given that she was in foster care as a baby. Fortunately, a loving couple adopted her and has been super-supportive of her desire to perform. She sang her first song at eighteen months, first appeared on stage at age six in a school talent show, and moved to Los Angeles (with her mom, dad, and sister) at age thirteen to follow her dreams.

Rachel got her break on the first season of *The X Factor*, where she made it to the top five before being let go in a public vote. Rachel took the loss in stride, though. And for Rachel, simply appearing on the show has been a win for her career! But Rachel doesn't take her good fortune for granted. Instead, she plans to start a foundation to help foster kids pursue their dreams!

# Carly Rose Sonenclar

**Name:** Carly Rose Sonenclar
**Birthday:** April 20, 1999
**Hometown:** Mamaroneck, New York
**Parents:** Bob Sonenclar and Terri Edelman Sonenclar
**Sibling:** older brother, Russell
**Pet:** none (She used to have a blue lobster but it died!)
**Favorite Foods:** chicken, pasta, pot roast, chili
**Favorite Musicians:** Nina Simone, Etta James
**Hobbies:** playing sports, cooking

It's ironic that Carly Rose Sonenclar ended up on the American version of *The X Factor*, since her first musical "performances" involved pretending she was on *American Idol* at age two! A few years later, Carly Rose's parents enrolled her in music, acting, and dance classes. One of her teachers recognized Carly Rose's talent and put her in touch with an agent in nearby New York City. Carly Rose got her start in theatre, with one of her first roles being Young Cosette in Broadway's *Les Misérables*.

Before appearing on *The X Factor*, she also had minor roles in two movies.

In 2012, she auditioned for the second season of *The X Factor*. Her soulful performance caused notoriously tough judge Simon Cowell to stand up and applaud. In fact, all four judges gave her the thumbs-up. Her powerful voice—guest mentor will.i.am called her "possessed"—helped her advance to the finale, where the thirteen-year-old was pitted against thirty-seven-year-old Tate Stevens.

Despite the fervor of her fans, who call themselves "Carly's Angels," she didn't garner enough votes to win. But this runner-up didn't do so badly: Her videos on YouTube have received over twenty million views, and chances are this tremendously talented teen will have a record deal before long!

# Cassadee Pope

## ★ STAR STATS ★

**Name:** Cassadee Blake Pope
**Birthday:** August 28, 1989
**Hometown:** West Palm Beach, Florida
**Favorite Musicians:** Michelle Branch,
Avril Lavigne, Blink182, Four Year
Strong, Taylor Swift, Kelly Clarkson
**Hobbies:** cooking, hiking, writing

Cassadee Pope almost didn't audition for *The Voice*. In fact, she turned down the opportunity the first time it came around. Back then, she was already the lead singer of a somewhat successful punk band called Hey Monday, and she had also gone on tour as a solo acoustic act. Cassadee wanted to establish herself the old-fashioned way.

By the time *The Voice* began auditions for the third season, however, Cassadee was struggling

financially and finding it more challenging than she'd expected to get her solo career off the ground. So she decided to give the show a go, and it's a good thing she did! In December 2012, she became the youngest person and the first female to ever win *The Voice*.

Following the show, she signed a recording contract and went into the studio to work on a solo album to be released in 2013. On it, she'll showcase some of the country music chops she gained by working with her *Voice* mentor Blake Shelton. With this project ahead of her, she now says that going on *The Voice* was the best career decision she ever made. It's hard to believe she almost didn't do it!

# China Anne McClain

**Name:** China Anne McClain
**Birthday:** August 25, 1998
**Hometown:** Decatur, Georgia
**Parents:** Michael and Shontelle McClain
**Siblings:** older sisters Sierra and Lauryn; brother, Gabriel
**Pets:** a dog named Cujo
**Favorite Books:** The Hunger Games series, Twilight series
**Hobbies:** singing, dancing, drawing, reading, crocheting, Rollerblading

On the Disney show *A.N.T. Farm*, China Anne McClain plays a teen with extraordinary musical talent — a role that's not much of a stretch! Like her character, she sings and plays several instruments, including bass, piano, guitar, and violin.

With her dad working as a music producer and her mom as a songwriter, China has been performing music from a young age. Her acting career, however, happened by chance. One day she sang for a well-connected family friend who, after hearing her croon, recommended her for a part in a musical movie called *The Gospel*. She got the gig and loved it. From there, she landed a recurring role on the TV series *Tyler Perry's House of Payne*. Then in 2010, she was cast on *A.N.T. Farm*. China has also acted in the 2010 Adam Sandler comedy *Grown Ups*, as well as the sequel, which is due out in 2013.

Meanwhile, China has been further exercising her vocal cords as part of the McClain Sisters, a band she's formed with her older sibs, Sierra and Lauryn. The girls—who acted together in the 2007 movie *Daddy's Little Girls*—released their first single "Go" in November 2012; their debut album is expected to drop this year.

# Jaden Smith

**Name:** Jaden Christopher Syre Smith
**Birthday:** July 8, 1998
**Hometown:** Malibu, California
**Parents:** Will Smith and Jada Pinkett Smith
**Siblings:** younger sister, Willow; older half brother, Trey
**Pet:** a bulldog named Little Homie
**Hobbies:** skateboarding

**J**aden Smith's first movie role was opposite his actor dad Will Smith in the 2006 film *The Pursuit of Happyness*, when he was just five years old. This year, he had another chance to work with his famous father, in the June sci-fi release *After Earth*. It's no surprise, then, that Jaden says his dad has taught him a lot about acting.

Another thing he has in common with his dad— as well as his mom, Jada Pinkett Smith, and sister, Willow—is an interest in music. He rapped on Justin Bieber's song "Never Say Never," which was on the soundtrack for the 2010 remake *The Karate*

*Kid* in which Jaden starred. Since filming the video together, Jaden guested on a few more of the pop star's tracks, and even joined the Biebs on several stops of his Believe tour. (Now the two are BFFs!) Jaden's released a few singles of his own, including the 2013 song "Kite," which features Willow.

While he doesn't yet have an album out, Jaden put out a free rap "mixtape" in October 2012, composed of both remixes and original music. He's also launching a clothing line with skater style called Msfts. And he's a youth ambassador for Project Zambia, a program that helps AIDS orphans in Africa.

# One Direction

## Niall Horan
### STAR STATS

**Name:** Niall James Horan
**Birthday:** September 13, 1993
**Hometown:** Mullingar, County Westmeath, Ireland
**Parents:** Maura Gallagher and Bobby Horan
**Sibling:** older brother, Greg
**Musical Influences:** Michael Bublé, The Eagles, Bon Jovi, The Script

## Zayn Malik
### STAR STATS

**Name:** Zayn Javadd Malik
**Birthday:** January 12, 1993
**Hometown:** Bradford, West Yorkshire, England
**Parents:** Yaser and Tricia Malik
**Siblings:** older sister, Doniya; younger sisters Waliyha and Safaa
**Musical Influences:** *NSYNC

# Liam Payne
## ★ STAR STATS ★

**Name:** Liam James Payne
**Birthday:** August 29, 1993
**Hometown:** Wolverhampton, West Midlands, England
**Parents:** Karen and Geoff Payne
**Siblings:** older sisters Ruth and Nicola
**Musical Influences:** Justin Timberlake, Gary Barlow

# Harry Styles
## ★ STAR STATS ★

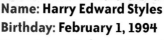

**Name:** Harry Edward Styles
**Birthday:** February 1, 1994
**Hometown:** Holmes Chapel, Cheshire, England
**Parents:** Anne Cox and Des Styles; stepfather, Robin Twist
**Sibling:** older sister, Gemma
**Musical Influences:** Elvis Presley, the Beatles, Foster the People, Coldplay, Kings of Leon

# Louis Tomlinson
## ★ STAR STATS ★

**Name:** Louis William Tomlinson
**Birthday:** December 24, 1991
**Hometown:** Doncaster, South Yorkshire, England
**Parents:** Johannah Poulston and Troy Austin; stepfather, Mark Tomlinson
**Siblings:** Georgia Austin; Charlotte, Félicité, Daisy, and Phoebe Tomlinson
**Musical Influences:** The Fray, The Killers, Ed Sheeran

Can you imagine a world *without* One Direction? The funny thing is that the group wouldn't even have been a group had they not all separately auditioned for the seventh season of *The X Factor* in the UK. One of the judges suggested they might do better as a group, and the rest is history!

While the band didn't win—they placed third—they walked away with a recording contract on Simon Cowell's record label and a passionate fan base. Their album *Up All Night* was released in America in March 2012, and the group went on to become the first British band to have their debut album enter the US charts in the number-one slot. In September 2012, they won three MTV Video Music Awards, including one for Best New Artist.

The guys quickly got back into the studio. Their second album, *Take Me Home*, dropped in November 2012, and their third album, *Where We Are*, will be available by Christmas 2013. To celebrate, the band kicks off a worldwide stadium tour in the spring of 2014. Fans can't wait to see what these cuties will be up to next!

# Cymphonique

**Name:** Cymphonique Miller
**Birthday:** August 1, 1996
**Hometown:** Los Angeles, California
**Parent:** Percy Robert Miller (aka Master P)
**Siblings:** eight half or step siblings, including Romeo (aka Masarati Romeo)
**Pets:** a Chihuahua named Honey Angel
**Favorite Food:** frozen yogurt
**Favorite Actress:** Zoe Saldana
**Hobbies:** kickboxing, swimming, drawing, playing the piano

As the star of the recent Nickelodeon series *How to Rock*, Cymphonique played a high schooler who starts a band in hopes of becoming popular. Music is a subject this Los Angeles native knows a thing or two about: After all, her dad is rapper and producer Master P, and her brother is Masarati Romeo (who you may remember as Lil' Romeo—he's not so little anymore!). Plus, she has an R&B singing career all her own. She's released a few singles, which have played on Radio Disney;

she's toured with the likes of Demi Lovato, Ashley Tisdale, and Raven-Symoné; and she's been nominated for Best Female Hip-Hop Artist at the BET Awards.

As for her acting career, Cymphonique guest starred on a few Nick shows before being cast in *How to Rock*. The funny thing is that she got that part by trying out at an open audition, and those doing the casting didn't know who she was or that her brother had his own Nick show! When she's not performing, she's doing acts of kindness: Her charity, Fabulous Girls Charity, raises awareness about children's cancer, and she's also helping build a school focused on performing arts.

# Logan Lerman

**Name:** Logan Wade Lerman
**Birthday:** January 19, 1992
**Hometown:** Beverly Hills, California
**Parents:** Lisa and Larry Lerman;
stepmom, Marilyn Silver
**Siblings:** older sister, Lindsey; older
brother, Lucas; stepsister, Laura Silver
**Pets:** two dogs named Lola and Stella
**Favorite Food:** sushi
**Favorite Movies:** *Eternal Sunshine of
the Spotless Mind, The Life Aquatic
with Steve Zissou*
**Hobbies:** playing music, soccer

Logan Lerman grew up in Beverly Hills and told his mother at age two and a half that he was planning to be an actor! Soon after that he started doing commercials, and he had his first movie role at the ripe age of eight. Since then, Logan has built up an impressive film resumé, which includes starring roles in *Hoot*, *The Three Musketeers*, and, of course, the fantasy flick *Percy Jackson & the Olympians: The Lightning Thief*. He also appeared

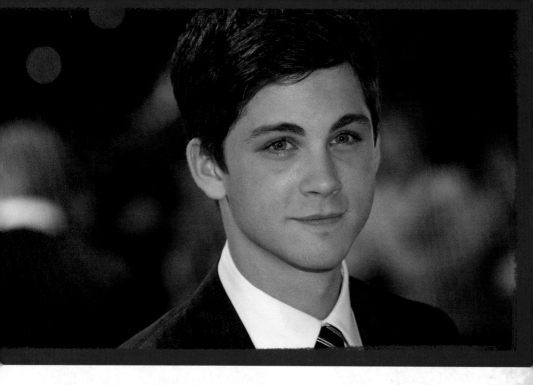

in the sequel *Percy Jackson: Sea of Monsters*, based on the second of the five books in the fantasy series, which came out in August 2013. (Lerman has said he's open to appearing in all five films.) He also has a prominent role in *Noah*, a film based on the Bible story that's set to release in 2014. One day, this self-described "film geek" would like to make his own movies and perhaps even head a studio!

In his spare time, Logan plays guitar, piano, bass, violin, and ukulele. He writes songs, too, and has played in a band with fellow actor Dean Collins.

# Diamond White

**Name: Diamond White**
**Birthday: January 1, 1999**
**Hometown: Detroit, Michigan**
**Parent: Deborah White**
**Pet: a dog named Pepsi**
**Favorite Food: ice cream and fries—**
**together**
**Favorite Musicians: Beyoncé, Justin**
**Bieber, Cher Lloyd, Nicki Minaj,**
**Whitney Houston**

Singer Diamond White grew up in Detroit and was raised by a single mom. The first notes she ever sang were along with the television while watching *Barney & Friends* when she was just nine months old!

She gave her first *real* performance at age six when she sang the national anthem for her elementary school's graduation. Diamond soon secured some stage roles, including one in a touring production of *The Color Purple*. Diamond and her mom eventually moved to Los Angeles, where they shared a one-bedroom apartment so Diamond could pursue her career. She soon landed some cartoon voiceover work for *Phineas and Ferb* and *Transformers: Rescue Bots*.

After seeing the first season of *The X Factor US*, Diamond knew she wanted to audition. Her performance wowed the judges, and she was selected for the second season's teen category. Though she was sent home early on, she was brought back as a wildcard. After advancing to the top six, however, she was sent home a second time in December 2012.

Though she'd hoped for the best, Diamond says she was still happy with her fifth place finish. That positive attitude will likely propel her toward her next goals: recording an album, continuing to pursue an acting career, and eventually becoming a "mogul"!

# Justin Bieber

In the last twelve months, Justin Bieber released *Believe Acoustic*, his seventh full-length album and his fifth to top the music charts; he's been on a concert tour, for which he sold out all his North American dates in an hour flat; he became the most-followed person on Twitter; *and* he hosted *Saturday Night Live*. Wow! What a year!

To think that his ever-surging career all started with a YouTube video his mother posted of the twelve-year-old Bieber singing in a local talent

competition. Inspired by reactions from strangers, Justin posted more. A few months later, pop manager Scooter Braun accidentally happened upon Bieber's channel. Impressed, he flew Bieber to Atlanta to record a demo and meet singer Usher. Soon after, Bieber signed with Island Records, in partnership with Braun and Usher. The label has put out all of his albums thus far, including *My World*, *My World 2.0*, *Under the Mistletoe*, *Believe*, and *Believe Acoustic*.

When he's not on the Believe tour or hanging with pals (Jaden Smith ranks among his besties), the Biebs is already thinking about his next album. With his fervent Beliebers behind him, he'll likely find himself at the top of the charts again in no time.

# Emblem3

## Wesley Stromberg
### ★ STAR STATS ★

**Name:** Wesley Trent Stromberg
**Birthday:** December 6, 1993
**Parents:** Laraine Claire and William Stromberg
**Siblings:** younger brother, Keaton; sisters Brooke and Brianna

## Keaton Stromberg
### ★ STAR STATS ★

**Name:** Keaton Robert Stromberg
**Birthday:** July 16, 1996
**Parents:** Laraine Claire and William Stromberg
**Siblings:** older brother, Wesley; sisters Brooke and Brianna

## Drew Chadwick
### ★ STAR STATS ★

**Name:** Andrew Michael Chadwick
**Birthday:** October 1, 1992
**Hometown (for all):** Sequim, Washington
**Musical Influences:** Blink 182, Incubus, the Beatles, Red Hot Chili Peppers, Sublime
**Hobbies:** surfing, skateboarding, snowboarding, watching *SpongeBob SquarePants*

Don't call Emblem3 a boy band! The trio, which finished fourth in the second season of the American *The X Factor*, would rather be thought of as musicians. Unlike most boy bands, they write their own songs—one of which they performed for their audition—and play the instruments on their tracks. Their signature style is a combination of hip-hop, alternative rock, and reggae.

Brothers Wesley and Keaton, and their buddy Drew began playing music together as preteens growing up in Sequim, Washington. (The Strombergs come from a musical family: Their dad composes film and TV scores, and their mom is a professional harpist.) The three friends were known as The American Scholars, and Keaton, Wes, and Drew self-produced an album when they were nine, eleven, and thirteen respectively.

When Wes was sixteen, he moved to Huntington Beach, California, to further his music career; not long after, he convinced his bandmates to follow. Even before they auditioned for *The X Factor*, they were beginning to have success booking gigs, but the show made them a household name. Though the trio was eliminated in Week Seven, their mentor didn't give up on them! Since the show aired, the group has released a debut single, "Chloe (You're The One I Want)" and started recording an album with Simon Cowell's record label, Syco. Surely, it won't be long before fans hear from these three musicians again!